GW00707862

# STEPS

Cynthia Spell Humbert
Betty Blaylock
Dr. Frank Minirth

A
JANET
THOMA
BOOK

THOMAS NELSON PUBLISHERS
Nashville

*We admitted we were
powerless over our
dependencies—that our lives
had become
unmanageable.*
**—Step One**

You can only get help by being honest about your powerlessness.

*I can do all things through Christ who strengthens me.*
**—Philippians 4:13**

When God gives us a job to do, he also provides the power to get the job done.

*A man should never be
ashamed to own he has
been in the wrong, which is
but saying, in other words,
that he is wiser today than
he was yesterday.*
**—Alexander Pope**

In each problem area of our lives, we tend to try to grab the reins of control. Success comes when we submit to God and allow him to have control.

*Turn Yourself to me, and
have mercy on me,
For I am desolate and
afflicted.*
**—Psalm 25:16**

Surrendering to a sense of powerlessness is not easy, but it is a beginning. God will never leave you alone.

*We came to believe that a
Power greater than ourselves
could restore us to sanity.*
**—Step Two**

When we are consumed by addiction, we have given our heart, soul, and mind to a false god. Only one true God is worthy of our heart, soul, and mind, and he is able to restore us.

"For I know the thoughts
that I think toward you, says
the LORD, thoughts of peace
and not of evil, to give you a
future
and a hope."
—*Jeremiah 29:11*

God promises us a future
that is rich with hope. He
has never backed out on a
single promise.

*Whenever I am afraid,*
*I will trust in you.*
**—Psalm 56:3**

Changes in our lives may be scary at times. We can cling to God like a frightened child holds onto a trusted parent. God always supports us, and his love never fails.

*Jesus said to him, "If you can believe, all things are possible to him who believes."*

**—Mark 9:23**

God offers us faith that can perform miracles, faith that when we are down, we can reach up to him, and he will give us the strength to try again. All we have to do is believe in him.

*We made a decision to turn
our will and our lives over to
the care of God as we
understood Him.*

**—Step Three**

Lord, help me decide to
leave things in your hands.

Don't quit five minutes
before the miracle happens.
                    **—Anonymous**

We often are discouraged
by our small steps in
maturing, but we can trust
that God eventually will
produce a masterpiece.

*Cast your burden on the
LORD,
And He shall sustain you;
He shall never permit the
righteous to be moved.*
**—Psalm 55:22**

Many times I put things in
God's hands, only to take
them back again. He can
be trusted to sustain my life.

*I lay down and slept;*
*I awoke, for the LORD*
*sustained me.*
*I will not be afraid of ten*
*thousands of people*
*Who have set themselves*
*against me all around.*
*—Psalm 3:5–6*

Sometimes my tasks seem insurmountable. When I trust God for guidance and commit my projects to him, despair turns into hope, and I feel less overwhelmed. I can rest in his love.

*We made a searching and
fearless moral inventory
of ourselves.*

**—Step Four**

Do we dare stand in front of a mirror and ask God to reveal our true selves to us, when we spend most of our time denying who we really are?

*I will fear no evil;*
*For You are with me.*
**—Psalm 23:4**

A journey through our darkest places feels painful and scary, but the search must be made. The promise of God is to be with us always. We can trust in him.

*Just as He chose us in Him before the foundation of the world, that we should be holy and without blame before Him in love.*
**—Ephesians 1:4**

Jesus calls us to look at our sins, not dwell on them. He tells us that God loves us exactly where we are. In his eyes we are perfect, because his love has brought us forgiveness.

*Let us search out and
examine our ways,
And turn back to the LORD.*
**—Lamentations 3:40**

We usually want to avoid looking at our root issues. It seems easier to deal with surface symptoms, but as long as the roots remain buried, symptoms will resurface.

*We admitted to God, to ourselves, and to another human being the exact nature of our wrongs.*
**—Step Five**

Keeping secrets makes us sick. They form abscessed wounds in our hearts, and we move into addictions to try to stop the pain. As we voice the secrets, they lose their power over us, and our hearts can begin to heal.

*That we should no longer be children, tossed to and fro and carried about with every wind of doctrine, by the trickery of men, in the cunning craftiness by which they lie in wait to deceive.*

**—Ephesians 4:14**

Even when the winds of change threaten us, God has everything under control. The more we practice placing our trust in God, the less we struggle with the winds.

*The steps of a good man are
ordered by the Lord,
And He delights in his way.*
**—Psalm 37:23**

By planning ahead rather than acting impulsively, and relying on the power of God rather than our own power, we can handle stress.

*And Jesus answered them and said to them, "Those who are well do not need a physician, but those who are sick."*

**—Luke 5:31**

We wear masks every day to keep people from knowing us. We fear that if others knew us they would abandon us, yet continuing to wear the masks keeps us apart from intimate relationships.

*We were entirely ready to
have God remove all these
defects of character.*

**—Step Six**

Holding a grudge breeds
bitterness. Carrying
resentment is like dragging
around an anchor. It tires us
out and steals the joy of
living. Bitterness damages us
more than the people we
are angry with.

*For the message of the cross is foolishness to those who are perishing, but to us who are being saved it is the power of God.*
**—1 Corinthians 1:18**

In our imperfection we move away from God, but in his perfection he is always with us, pursuing us, loving us, forgiving us, and giving us hope.

"For if you forgive men their trespasses, your heavenly Father will also forgive you. But if you do not forgive men their trespasses, neither will your Father forgive your trespasses."
—*Matthew 6:14–15*

We do not forgive because
the other person deserves
forgiveness; we forgive
because we deserve
freedom from anger.

*We humbly asked God to
remove our shortcomings.*
**—Step Seven**

With God, we no longer rely
on our own strength to
change.

*As far as the east is from the west,
So far has He removed our transgressions from us.*
**—Psalm 103:12**

God must really care about us a lot to relieve us so completely no matter what we have done and what our weaknesses are.

*If we confess our sins, He is faithful and just to forgive us our sins and to cleanse us from all unrighteousness.*
**—1 John 1:9**

Thank goodness God is more gentle with us than we are with each other and ourselves. He helps us see the easy things to change first, then guides us through the more difficult problems.

*We made a list of all persons*
*we had harmed and*
*became willing to make*
*amends to them all.*
**—Step Eight**

We must be willing to admit our responsibility in relationships and make amends to those we have harmed.

''Then his master . . . said to him, 'You wicked servant! I forgave you all that debt because you begged me. Should you not also have had compassion on your fellow servant, just as I had pity on you?' ''
—*Matthew 18:32–33*

When we begin to grasp the fullness of God's mercy toward us, we become more willing to extend mercy to those who have harmed us.

Let each of you look out not only for his own interests, but also for the interests of others.
**—Philippians 2:4**

Relationships cannot grow if they are ignored. Treat them like fine jewels that are to be maintained and treasured.

"And just as you want men to do to you, you also do to them likewise."

**—Luke 6:31**

There are many ways to
seek amends. God just asks
for our willingness.

*We made direct amends to such people wherever possible, except when to do so would injure them or others.*
**—Step Nine**

Our hearts feel lighter as we
mend past relationships.

*We love Him because He first loved us.*
**—1 John 4:19**

Only God can fully satisfy
our need for love, but the
people in our lives are our
greatest opportunity to show
his love to others and to
experience his love (through
human form) for us.

*Forgiveness is a gift I give myself.*
**—Anonymous**

We become victims of
ourselves when we choose
not to forgive others.

*We continued to take
personal inventory, and
when we were wrong,
promptly admitted it.*
**—Step Ten**

Our shortcomings are a part of who we are. We all have them. We need daily to ask God for insight into our own thoughts and behavior so we can begin to change them with his guidance.

*For it is God who works in
you both to will and to do
for His good pleasure.*
**—Philippians 2:13**

Success cannot be achieved
by our will, but by the might
and power of God working
in us.

*There are defeats more triumphant than victories.*
**—Montaigne**

If we learn from our defeat,
it can become a victory that
leads us forward.

*The people we relate to
need to know we have
boundaries. It will help them
and us.*
**—Melody Beattie**

People can learn to respect us, and we can learn to trust ourselves when we start saying what we really mean.

*We sought through prayer and meditation to improve our conscious contact with God, as we understood Him, praying only for the knowledge of His will for us and the power to carry that out.*

**—Step Eleven**

The important difference
between our earthly
relationships and the one
we have with God is that he
doesn't change every time
we talk with him. He is
always the same and will
always be there when we
seek him.

*Seek (wisdom) as silver,
And search for (wisdom) as
for hidden treasures . . .*
**—Proverbs 2:4**

We must search for the
knowledge and
understanding of God as we
would search for something
very precious.

*To everything there is a
season,
A time for every purpose
under heaven.*
**—Ecclesiastes 3:1**

We gain patience as we live
life one step at a time.

"I have come as a light into the world, that whoever believes in Me should not abide in darkness."
—**John 12:46**

We no longer need to fear
the darkness when we walk
in God's light.

*Having had a spiritual awakening as the result of these steps, we tried to carry this message to others and to practice these principles in all our affairs.*

**—Step Twelve**

We need to share with others the power that is great enough to free us from our self-will, the power that can forgive and lead us to forgiveness of ourselves and others.

*And let us consider one another in order to stir up love and good works, not forsaking the assembling of ourselves together, as is the manner of some, but exhorting one another . . .*
**—Hebrews 10:24–25**

When we share our struggles with others who have the same problem, we help them and ourselves.

*Be still, and know that I am God.*
**—Psalm 46:10**

We can't all rush away for a
vacation when we are
stressed, but we can create
quiet moments right where
we are.

*Philip found Nathanael and said to him, "We have found Him . . . Jesus of Nazareth, the son of Joseph." And Nathanael said to him, "Can anything good come out of Nazareth?" Philip said to him, "Come and see."*
**—John 1:45–46**

There are many effective
witnessing methods, but
nothing so strong as a
simple invitation.

## The Twelve Steps of Alcoholics Anonymous

1. We admitted we were powerless over alcohol—that our lives had become unmanageable.
2. Came to believe that a Power greater than ourselves could restore us to sanity.
3. Made a decision to turn our will and our lives over to the care of God as we understood Him.
4. Made a searching and fearless moral inventory of ourselves.
5. Admitted to God, to ourselves, and to another human being the exact nature of our wrongs.
6. Were entirely ready to have God remove all these defects of character.
7. Humbly asked Him to remove our shortcomings.
8. Made a list of all persons we had harmed and became willing to make amends to them all.
9. Made direct amends to such people wherever possible, except when to do so would injure them or others.

10. Continued to take personal inventory and when we were wrong, promptly admitted it.

11. Sought through prayer and meditation to improve our conscious contact with God, as we understood Him, praying only for knowledge of His will for us and the power to carry that out.

12. Having had a spiritual awakening as the result of these steps, we tried to carry this message to alcoholics, and to practice these principles in all our affairs.

Published in Nashville, Tennessee, by Thomas
Nelson, Inc., and distributed in Canada by
Lawson Falle, Ltd., Cambridge, Ontario.

Scripture quotations are from the NEW KING
JAMES VERSION of the Bible. Copyright © 1979,
1980, 1982, Thomas Nelson, Inc., Publishers.

### Library of Congress
### Cataloging-in-Publication Data

Steps / by Cynthia Spell Humbert . . . (et al.).
    p.  cm.
''A Janet Thoma book.''
ISBN 0-8407-7814-7
   1. Twelve-step programs—Religious
aspects—Christianity.  I. Shoemaker, Sam.
BV4596.T88S84  1993
242'.4—dc20              92-37895
                         CIP

Printed in Singapore.
1 2 3 4 — 96 95 94 93